T0381141

Archway Publishing books may be ordered through booksellers or by contacting:

Archway Publishing
1663 Liberty Drive
Bloomington, IN 47403
www.archwaypublishing.com
844-669-3957

ISBN: 978-1-6657-7163-4 (sc)
978-1-6657-7165-8 (hc)
978-1-6657-7164-1 (e)

Library of Congress Control Number: 2025900509

Print information available on the last page.

Archway Publishing rev. date: 01/15/2025

THE WOLF

by

Dan Mena

The Wolf is a majestic, intelligent, productive, social animal. Wolves keep the environment clean and balanced. They do not harm humans. We need to understand and protect them as they have as much **right** to live on Planet Earth as we do! After all, they lived and were on Earth before we were! It's known that the lineage of the Gray Wolf goes back to some 2 million years. Yes, the Wolf has roamed our Planet for over **2 million years**!! Wolves live in the United States, Canada, Mexico, Europe, Russia, Greenland and Asia.

There are two types of Wolves that live in North America, the Gray Wolf and the Red Wolf. The Gray Wolf is the larger of the two. In this book, we will be discussing the behavior of the Gray Wolf, also known as the Timber Wolf. The Gray Wolf varies in color from pure white to solid black. The most common shade is a mixture of black, white, gold and brown fur. Their eyes also vary in color; from gold to orange; even green. Today, there are over 20,000 Gray Wolves living in the United States.

A full grown Gray Wolf

Wolves live in most of the states of our country, but prefer the Northwest best; states like Montana, North and South Dakota, Wyoming, Idaho and Colorado.

Wolves have two layers of fur; the outer or **guard layer** is made up of coarse hair which is water repellant.

The **inner layer** is made up of thick soft gray "wool" which insulates the Wolf from the cold air. This inner layer allows the Wolf to tolerate temperatures as low as 40F degrees below zero! **Now that's COLD!!**

The Wolf is so well insulated, that snow **does not melt** when it lands on its fur. In the springtime, as the cold air becomes warmer, the inner layer is shed to keep the Wolf cool as summer approaches.

A Gray Wolf sleeping in the snow

Most Wolves usually breed once a year, in the spring; March or April.

The Wolf is the only carnivore on our planet that does not mate with its

relatives. New born baby Wolves are called **PUPS.** One is shown below.

Pups are born in **Litters** in a **Den.** A Den is a cave dug into the earth by the

mother Wolf. A female Wolf takes up to 9 weeks or about 63 days for her

litter to be born. A litter can be from 4 to 10 pups in number.

Wolves are excellent parents; protecting and feeding their young.

Pups grow very fast and by the time 6 weeks have past, they are exploring the area around the Den. They play and have fun with their sisters and brothers. Pups grow to be about 5 feet long and 2 feet high. An adult male weighs 75 to 120 pounds; adult females weigh 60 to 95 pounds.

An adult full grown mature male Gray Wolf

Wolves are sociable animals that live and hunt in **packs.** A Wolf pack is a highly organized, complex social structure of 6 to 10 wolves, who are all family members.

The pack is made up of parents, siblings, siblings of earlier litters, and cousins from other packs who are adopted by the pack. Some packs can be as large as 17 Wolves! Pack members live within a disciplined order, with plenty of rules that must be obeyed!!

The Wolf is a carnivorous animal. Wolves eat deer, elk, buffalo, caribou and moose. A pack will travel 50 to 125 miles in search of prey. They can trot at speeds of 10 miles per hour indefinitely when hunting and run as fast as 45 miles per hour when hunting down their prey.

Wolves can run fast both in deep snow and dry land because they have long slender legs and webbed feet. Their webbed feet also make them excellent swimmers. In addition, they can climb trees if they must.

Each member of the pack has a responsibility to the pack as they depend on one another for food. They are highly skilled predators. They kill their prey as a team.

The pack can control an area as large as 1000 square miles and as small as 14 to 20 square miles, which is called a **territory.** The pack will aggressively defend its territory from other Wolves.

The Wolf is a commanding **strategic** hunter. The pack will disperse a herd

of elk by attacking it in groups of 2 or 3 Wolves. They bring down the elk by

running behind it and biting through their legs. The jaw muscles of a Wolf

are twice as powerful as those of a German Shepard dog, and can produce

pressures of up to 1500 pounds per square inch. Together with their sharp teeth, they can cut through the leg bone of an elk or caribou on the first bite! They have 42 very sharp teeth.

Wolves also bring down elk and other prey by a) biting the prey's soft underbelly, which causes bleeding and b) by running up to the front of their prey, biting into the nose or throat of the prey and hanging on with their powerful teeth until the prey goes down!

The leaders of the pack are the dominant male and dominant female, or the Alpha Male and the Alpha Female called the **Alpha pair.** The Alpha pair stands to their full height, carrying their heads and tails high. The rest of the pack keep their heads down and walk with their tails between their legs when in the company of the Alpha pair.

Above is an Alpha male and an Alpha female or the Alpha Pair. The Alpha male only mates with the Alpha female. He does not mate with the other members of his family. The Alpha pair decides when the pack will travel and hunt. They are normally the first to feed after a kill.

Mature male Wolves, who wish to mate, must leave the pack and seek a mate. They will leave their birth pack after 2 or 4 years in search of a female with which to mate to establish their own pack and territory.

When a Wolf, mates and forms his own pack, he may encounter in the wild, a brother, a sister or a cousin from his birth pack.

They recognize each other when they meet. They wag their tails, lick their faces, rub their heads together or stand on their hind legs, placing their front legs on each other's shoulders as if hugging! The Wolf is the only carnivore on planet Earth that performs in this manner.

Wolves defending their territory from other packs usually will not fight to the death. They will draw back their lips showing their big teeth. They growl and sneer to frighten the intruder away.

The lesser ranking Wolf will give in and leave. This behavior prevents killing each other which keeps the number of Wolves in each pack increasing instead of decreasing.

The lesser ranking Wolf giving in.

Wolves communicate in many ways, as the Alpha pair does with the pack. They pucker their lips as if talking. They also have a keen sense of smell that allows them to recognize each other and prey from a distance.

Howling is another way Wolves communicate. Wolves enjoy howling. Howling is a form of greeting and a call to other Wolves. They howl to bring the pack together or to warn other packs of intruders. They also howl to attract a mate. A Wolf howl can be heard up to 10 miles on the open tundra.

Contrary to the myth, Wolves **DO NOT** howl at the moon!!

Gray Timber Wolf howling

Howling Timber Wolf pup

In the wild, Wolves live only 3 to 5 years. Protecting each other is most important to them. In captivity, they can live 10 to 15 years.

Wolves live short lives in the wild, because many die before their first birthday from disease or malnutrition. Others die from accidents or by being killed by the same animals they hunt, such as the moose or buffalo. However, the biggest enemy of the Wolf is us; we humans!

Wolves are very shy creatures and avoid all contact with humans. They do not attack people or eat human flesh. They stay away from humans, yet people have killed Wolves for their fur or for sport.

Humans have also destroyed many of the Wolves habitats. The Wolf must then go on to farms and kill sheep or cattle to survive. Farmers then want to kill the Wolf who is not at fault. The Wolf would rather be in the wild but the wild is being taken away from him. We must help the Wolf regain his habitat; his territory, his hunting ground.

By preying on deer, elk and buffalo, the Wolf helps other animals to live by providing them with food sources. The Wolf creates an abundance of food for eagles, coyotes, ravens, grizzlies and foxes.

Without the Wolf, deer, elk and buffalo herds become overpopulated. Overpopulation can cause overgrazing, destroying the plant base, making forests less habitable and suitable for other animals. The Wolf saved Yellowstone National Park when they were brought back to cull the herds of deer, elk and buffalo that were destroying the forests. Wolves keep the

forests in balance and the ecosystem healthy. Wolves are very productive,

useful creatures that we must protect from harm and extinction!

This is Chewie, a family dog. He is a descendent of the Wolf!!
The Wolf is the ancestor of every dog we own and love.
The Wolf is Chewie's family. Shouldn't you protect Chewie's
family the Wolf?

Bibliography

1. Carbyn, L.N. Editor 1983. *Wolves in Canada and Alaska: Their Status, Biology and Management.* Canadian Wild Life Service revised 1993.

2. Cosmosmith.com. *The North American Gray Wolf.* 1999-2002

3. Lee, David N.B. *Apache Tribe Rolls Out Red Carpet for Wolves.* Wildlife Conservation, July/August 2002, p.18.

4. Murie, Adolph (1944**).** *Wolves of Mount McKinley*. U.S. Department of the Interior, Park Service

5. North American Wolf Association. *About Wolves…*March 2002.

6. Photographs by *Monty Sloan*. Wolf Park, Battleground, Indiana.

7. Smith, Doug. *Wolf Pack Photograph*. Yellowstone Park Service.

8. Weaver, John (1978). *Wolves of Yellowstone*. U.S. Department of the Interior, Park Service.

9. Wolf Park Staff authored. 2017. *What are Wolves?* Research Paper. Wolf Park, Battleground, Indiana. www.wolfpark.org.